THE KAZAN' ICON OF THE

HISTORY, SERVICE, AND AKATHIST HYMN

This translation is dedicated to our all-holy Lady, the Mother of God in gratitude for her many benefactions toward the translator, and to the very Reverend Archpriest Vladimir Shishkoff and the faithful of his parish, the Church of Our Lady of Kazan' in Newark, New Jersey, for the love and support they have shown and continue to show him.

BX
577.5
.K3
1988

Published by
THE ST. JOHN OF KRONSTADT PRESS
Rt. 1 Box 205
Liberty, TN 37095

ISBN 0-912927 - 13 - 5
Second Printing, 1988

Cover illustration:
copy of an icon written by Fr. Theodore Jurewicz

"The Mother of God of Kazan'" ©1984
the "Service" ©1983
the "Akathist" ©1985,
all by Isaac E. Lambertsen

All materials in this volume were translated from the Russian and Church Slavonic by Isaac E. Lambertsen. Sources for materials compiled to form "The Icon of the Mother of God of Kazan'": *Tales from the Earthly Life of the All-holy Theotokos, Concerning her Miraculous Icons and her Great Mercies to the Human Race,* pp. 264-271 (Jordanville, NY: 1974); *Prolog,* Vol. I (Sept.-Nov.), pp. 185b-187a, & Vol. II (June-Aug.), pp. 477a-479b (Moscow: Synodal Press?, 1802); *Destroyed and Defiled Churches,* Samizdat, p. 138 (Frankfurt/Main, W. Germany: Possev-Verlag, 1980).

THE ICON OF THE MOTHER OF GOD
OF KAZAN'

Which the Holy Church Celebrates on
the 8th of July and the 22nd of October

The miraculous icon of the Mother of God of Kazan' is of great significance for the faithful of the Russian Orthodox Church, and enjoys unparalleled veneration among Russia's Orthodox families. One of the most magnificent cathedrals in Russia was erected in St. Petersburg and dedicated to this icon, and in it was housed one of the miraculous copies of the original icon. For the most part it is with copies of the Kazan' icon that young couples are blessed to marry, and, illumined with the serene light of icon lamps perpetually burning in children's rooms, the meek face of the Mother of God gazes down with love on growing children.

In Moscow, a cathedral dedicated to the Kazan' icon stood on historic Red Square, opposite the walls of the Kremlin, some twenty paces from the chapel which housed the Iveron Icon. This famous church and its lofty bell-tower were demolished in 1934 as part of Stalin's plan to "counteract blind admiration for that which is old." Now the site of the cathedral, which is located opposite the entrance to the GUM department store, is occupied by underground toilet facilities and has been planted with evergreen shrubs. (There are at least twenty public toilet facilities which have been erected by Soviet authorities over the sites of demolished churches and chapels in Moscow alone!)

The Kazan' campaign of Tsar Ivan the Terrible resembled a church procession. Its purpose, it would seem, was more to bring a new flock to Christ than to subject new territory to the tsar of Moscovy. Kazan' fell on the feast of the Protection of the Mother of God. The battlements were breached and the turrets of Kazan' surrendered at the moment when, during the liturgy which was being celebrated in the portable royal church, the deacon intoned the petition of the litany: "That every enemy and adversary may be subjugated and trampled under his feet." Entering Kazan' on the following day, the Tsar immediately broke ground for a cathedral dedicated to

1

the Annunciation of the all-holy Theotokos. The Tsar indicated sites for the erection of other churches as well, and the following year the Diocese of Kazan' was instituted and St. Gurius was sent there as its first bishop.

With the zealous spreading of the light of Christ by Bishop Gurius and his successor St. Germanus, the propagation of the Faith in Kazan' proceeded apace; but later Islam showed considerable opposition. It was at this time that the Mother of God was pleased to glorify her icon for the strengthening of Orthodoxy.

In the year 1579, after a terrible conflagration which reduced half of Kazan's kremlin, and the portion of the city proper which was adjacent to it, to ruins, the Moslems began vocally to insinuate that the Russians' God was ill-disposed towards the Russians and had used the fire to show his anger with them. "The Faith of Christ," remarks the chronicler, "became a proverb and a byword." Then the Lord manifested his mercy. Here is the account as it has been transmitted in the Slavonic language.

"In the year 7087 [1579], during the reign of the pious and Christ-loving Sovereign Tsar and Great Prince Ivan Vasilievich, Autocrat of All Russia, and while the Most Holy Anthony was Metropolitan of Moscow and All Russia, and while Jeremiah was Archbishop of Kazan', the revelation of this icon of the all-holy Theotokos took place in the city of Kazan' in the following manner, after the conflagration which took place that year in the city of Kazan', on the 23rd day of July. Not far from the place where the fire had burned, near the Church of St. Nicholas, which was known as Tulsky, stood the house of a certain soldier by the name of Daniel Onuchin; and a stone's throw therefrom the icon of the all-holy Theotokos appeared to the daughter of a certain soldier, [a girl] by the name of Matrona.

"[The Mother of God] commanded her to go into the city and tell the archbishop and the military authorities to come and take it up from the bosom of the earth; and she showed her the place where it was buried. The girl foolishly feared to say [ought about this], but in time she did tell her mother; yet her mother paid her no heed. Afterwards, the icon of the all-

2

holy Theotokos appeared again in a vision to the same virgin, and commanded her to inform [the archbishop and authorities] of the vision without hesitation. The girl not once, but many times, told her mother of the appearance of the icon, but to no avail. Later on, it chanced on a certain day that that maiden was sleeping in her home at noon-time. Suddenly she found herself in the midst of her courtyard. The icon of the all-holy Theotokos appeared to her in an awesome and fiery visage, emitting rays of exceeding dreadful fire, so that it seemed to her that she would be consumed by those radiant and luminous rays. And a fearsome voice issued forth from the icon, saying to the maiden: "If thou dost not obey my words and take mine icon from the bosom of the earth, I shall appear to another, and thou shalt lose thy life in a horrible manner!'

"The maiden was stricken with great terror by this awesome vision, and she fell to the ground like one dead, and lay there for many hours. Then, [awakening], she cried to her mother with a loud voice to go and inform the archbishop and the military commanders of that city of the icon of the all-holy Theotokos which had appeared to her, and she related to her all that had been said to her and all that she had heard from the holy icon, and pointed out to her the place [where it lay buried]. Her mother went straightway to the city, to the military commanders, and set the maiden before her and commanded her to recount herself what had happened with her. Then the virgin related to them all that had been said, and all that she had heard from the holy icon, and described the place which had been indicated to her. But they stuck fast in their unbelief, and paid her no heed.

"When the mother of the girl saw that nothing availed, she shed tears and, taking her daughter, went to the archbishop, where she related to him the words she had been told, and told him of the place she had been shown, that he might give the order to take up the holy icon. But the archbishop likewise paid no heed to what had been said by her, and sent her away without doing anything. The 8th of July was the day on which they went to the military authorities and the archbishop; and it was the seventh hour of the day.

3

"At the twelfth hour of the same day, the woman, taking up a mattock, went herself to the place indicated, and dug for a long time, but did not find that which she sought. Soon others also began to dig; and they excavated the whole site, but found nothing. Then the maiden who had received the command began to dig on the place where a stove had formerly been, and the rest joined her; and as they dug down to a depth of a little more than two cubits — O the wonder! — straightway there appeared the miraculous icon of the all-holy Theotokos, the Directress, [holding] her pre-eternal Infant, our Lord Jesus Christ, which was covered by a sleeve from a certain garment of a cherry color. The miraculous icon itself shone with a marvellous splendor, as though it had been freshly painted, and no particles of earth adhered to it at all. The maiden, taking up the all-honorable icon with fear, trembling and joy, set it up in that place.

"When the people of the city heard this, they hastened thither in a great multitude to see that most wondrous miracle, and they cried out, weeping and saying: "O Mistress, save us!" When word of this reached the archbishop and the foremost citizens of the city, that hierarch went straightway in procession with the cross, to the place where the miraculous icon had been discovered; and he was accompanied by his whole priestly assembly, and by the governors of the city, and a multitude of the people. And seeing the holy icon most splendidly radiant as a priceless treasure, they were greatly astonished, for they had nowhere seen an icon of such lineaments, and were at a loss what to think; and they were seized with joy, and with fear because of their unbelief. But the archbishop and the military commanders fell down before the miraculous icon and prayed, weeping, asking the mercy of the all-holy Theotokos for the offense of their unbelief.

"And all the people, hastening to see the most wondrous marvel, with tears and joyful soul praised God and the Theotokos for the discovery of that priceless treasure. Then the archbishop commanded that the holy icon, together with the other icons and the cross [which had been borne thither in procession], be taken to the nearby Church of St. Nicholas, known as Tulsky. And there, having celebrated services of supplication, the archbishop, together with all the sanctified assembly, and the leaders of the city, and with a multitude of men, together with women and children, followed the holy icons into the city, and they hastened after the newly-revealed miraculous icon. Indeed, trampling each other underfoot, some treading upon the heads of others, they strove to touch the wonderworking image. At that time the all-holy Lady and Mistress, the Theotokos, showed forth a miracle through her icon, and healed a poor man by the name of Joseph, who had completely lost his sight three years before. Beholding this marvel at that time, the people's love increased all the more. And bearing it into [the city], they placed it in the cathedral church of the all-holy Theotokos, [dedicated to] her honored and glorious Annunciation. There also the all-holy Theotokos healed the eyes of a certain man by the name of Nicetas, whose sight was impaired. And after they had chanted services of supplication in the cathedral church, they dispersed to their homes, with fear and great joy.

"In the morning, after the archbishop had served the liturgy, the people again assembled in the holy cathedral church, and offered many gifts to the miraculous image: some giving gold, others silver, and others something else, each giving according to his means. Then the archbishop, the military commanders, and all the people, having had a copy made of the miraculous icon and recorded in writing its revelation and the miracles [wrought through it], sent [the copy and the report] to the royal city of Moscow, to the autocratic Sovereign Tsar and Great Prince Ivan Vasilievich, Autocrat of all Russia, and his sons; and they, seeing it, marvelled exceedingly at its unique lineaments. Then the pious Sovereign Tsar and Great Prince and his sons commanded that a church, dedicated to the all-holy Theotokos, the honored Directress, be constructed of wood on the place where that miraculous icon was found, and that a convent be founded [there also], and that substantial alms be distributed [to the poor] from their own royal treasuries. And they ordered that an annual revenue be given to the sacred

5

assembly, to the abbess and forty nuns, which was done. In time, this precious, newly-revealed icon of the all-holy Theotokos was brought with honor to the convent, with supplicatory hymnody, accompanied by the archbishop and nobles, and all the people..." (Prolog, Vol. II, pp. 477a-479b [Moscow: Synodal Press?, 1802]).

The maiden Matrona and her mother were the first to receive the tonsure in the newly-built convent. Not long after the first, wooden, church, a new church of stone was constructed, with a refectory. In 1594 this church, too, was dismantled, and in the following year a new and spacious cathedral, dedicated to the Dormition of the Mother of God, was consecrated at the convent by Metropolitan Hermogenes.

The number of nuns in the sisterhood was then increased to sixty-four; and substantial endowments were made to the convent, in the form of ecclesiastical appointments, icons and vestments; the icon itself was clad with a magnificent covering of gold, studded with precious stones and pearls, a gift of the Tsar. New and splendid adornments were donated to the icon by the Empress Catherine II. And during her reign it was decided to replace the old cathedral, which had stood for two centuries and had become dilapidated, with a new one. In 1798, on Catherine's orders, 25,000 rubles were allocated for the construction, and it was consecrated in 1808.

The mind of the believer is involuntarily struck by a certain coincidence. The revelation of the Kazan' icon was itself a symbol of the triumph of Orthodox Russia over Islam. All during the time that cherished object was venerated in Kazan', the Russian Empire was at peace with the Orient. But on the night of June 29, 1904, several sacrilegious men broke into the cathedral church of the Kazan' convent and, stealing the miraculous Kazan' icon, took it away with them. The thieves were apprehended, but the icon vanished without a trace. At that time, the Russian forces suffered defeat at the hands of the Japanese in the East.

There are two opinions as to the fate of the original Kazan' icon. Some maintain that the original icon was kept in

Moscow and had been transferred thither in accordance with the desire of the Tsar, the move being kept secret so as not to distress the inhabitants of Kazan'. The Russian tsars loved to concentrate the holy objects of all places in Moscow. It is also possible that Metropolitan Hermogenes, at the time of his transfer to the patriarchal throne, brought the icon with him from Kazan'. When the capitol was moved to St. Petersburg, proponents of this opinion aver, it was this icon that was transferred to the new capitol with a number of other holy objects; consequently, the icon which was enshrined in the Kazan' Cathedral in St. Petersburg was the original.

Others are of the opinion that the original Kazan' icon was that which accompanied the army of Prince Pozharsky, and, on arriving in Moscow, remained in the cathedral constructed for it by Pozharsky on Red Square. But the dimensions of this icon are significantly smaller than those of the one which used to be in Kazan' and the one which was enshrined in St. Petersburg. Whatever the case, all three icons were shown to be great sources of the grace of the Mother of God.

The Petersburg Kazan' icon was the most cherished and beloved object of veneration in the capitol. Pilgrims stood constantly before it in prayer, and many of St. Petersburg's workers went every day to venerate the icon with a living sense of piety, taking a moment from the multitude of their concerns to greet, as it were, their Mother.

In the Kazan' Cathedral of St. Petersburg, Kutuzov rests the sleep of the dead after his historic and immortal labors. In 1812, heeding the voice of the people who demanded that Kutuzov be placed at the head of the Russian army, Emperor Alexander I, the Blessed, appointed him commander-in-chief. Before departing to join the forces, Kutuzov went to pray in the Kazan' Cathedral. The people unharnessed the horses from his carriage and cried out: "Drive out the French!" After a service of supplication was chanted, the Kazan' icon was placed on the head of Kutuzov, who was renowned for his piety. The Mother of God did not disappoint the hope placed in her by the chief general, and the field marshall returned in his coffin, surrounded with glory undimmed, to rest in the Kazan' Cathedral.

7

There is another monument from this period: the magnificent iconostasis cast of silver. The silver from which this was fashioned was recovered by the Cossacks from the French, who had looted it from the Churches of Moscow, and given as a gift to the Kazan' Cathedral. Under the miraculous image, in golden letters, one could read the short but expressive inscription: "Fervent offering of the Host of the Don." The origin of the icon in the Kazan' Cathedral in Moscow is as follows. It was sent from Kazan' to Prince Pozharsky, who was marching to liberate Moscow with an army assembled from northern cities. This was a difficult time in the history of the Russian realm. The last scion of the dynasty of Rurik, Tsar Basil Ivanovich Shuisky, had been deposed in 1606, and with him the royal line came to an end in Russia. An interregnum ensued, accompanied by divers depredations, tumults, violence and injustices.

At that time there appeared in Astrakhan, at the mouth of the Volga, a pretender, who gave himself out to be the Tsarevich Dimitri, who had been slain in Uglich. He drew many Cossacks to his side and great mobs of credulous people. To crown the misfortunes which befell the Russian land, the ancient capitol of Moscow was treacherously seized by Poles, who had brought to submission many other Russian cities as well. The Swedes also threatened the land from the north and had already annexed the city of Novgorod. Both the Poles and the Swedes wished to occupy Holy Russia once and for all, and to set up their own tsar to rule the Russian people.

The turmoil was so great and such anarchy ruled everywhere, that the majority of the Russian people, who longed for a cessation of the civil conflict and bloodshed, agreed to the imposition of the Polish Prince Wladislaw as their ruler. But the faithful children of Russia and the Orthodox Church would not consent to such a concession, which had no precedent in their history, viz., that a foreigner and heterodox person would rule the Orthodox Russian nation. The Russian people then came together and heroically rose up in defense of their royal city and homeland.

From all quarters of the vast land regiments and

companies of volunteers moved toward Moscow. Among the others there arrived from Nizhny-Novgorod a troop mustered by Prince Pozharsky, a mighty force in strength and faith. This regiment carried with it a copy of the miraculous Kazan' icon of the Mother of God, which belonged to the Prince.

With great trust in the aid of the Queen of heaven, the Russian host launched itself at the enemy, and the heavenly Mistress did not forsake her faithful servants. The insurgents wrested from the enemy the Novodevichy Convent, which the Poles had fortified, and captured a great many of the foe. Yet, although the enemy experienced repeated defeats inflicted upon them by the Russian forces, the ultimate salvation of Russia from the oppression of the foreigners did not ensue. Following the successes of the Russian army, disputes arose between its leaders. The Cossacks and other militiamen began to debauch themselves in drunkenness and indulged themselves in plundering and oppressing the surrounding inhabitants.

In 1611, in wintertime, the Kazan' icon of the Mother of God was sent back from Moscow to Kazan'. Along the way, the precious image was met in Yaroslavl' by the Nizhegorod regiment mustered by Minin, which was to submit to the command of Prince Pozharsky. This regiment, learning of the miracles manifested in Moscow through the aid of the Mother of God, took the icon with it and kept it constantly in their camp. The prayers of the Orthodox to the Queen of heaven for the salvation of the Russian land were heard by the all-pure Virgin. And the Mother of God spread her protecting veil of mercy over the suffering country.

Many obstacles were encountered by the Nizhegorod army when it arrived in Moscow. They had to capture a city well-fortified and stubbornly defended by the Poles, to drive out the fresh and sizeable Polish army which had arrived in that city, and to put down the riotous behavior and anarchy of the Russian troops. The gravity of the position was rendered more serious by the fact that because of the desolate condition of the surrounding area, supplies could not be obtained for the Russian forces. All of this caused cowardice and timidity to surface in the hearts of the soldiers.

Many of the devoted sons of Russia, despairing of being able to save their homeland by might of main, cried aloud in great grief: "Forgive us, O our homeland! Forgive us, sacred Kremlin! We have done all we can to liberate you, but it is clear that God is not pleased to bless our arms with victory!"

In such a lamentable situation, only hope for help from on high remained. With compunction of heart all the people and the soldiers began to send up entreaties to the all-holy Theotokos, begging her merciful intercession before the throne of her Son and our God. To intensify their prayerful appeals, in addition to serving a solemn service of supplication, all decided to keep a strict fast for three days. The Lord hearkened to the sorrowful cry of His faithful servants and showed forth His mercy upon the Orthodox Church and the Russian land. While the Russian forces prayed fervently to the Mother of God, entreating her aid in rescuing the capitol, the Poles blockaded themselves in the Kitai Gorod, having surrounded the Kremlin with a tight circle of fortifications. Inside the Kremlin, the Greek Archbishop Arsenius languished in Polish captivity. Here is the account of what transpired, as it has been transmitted in the Slavonic language:

"After the death of the pious Tsar and Great Prince Basil Ivanovich [Shuisky] of All Russia, the great royal city of Moscow was captured by impious Poles, because of our sins. Then all the armies of the various cities of the Russian land marched to [its aid], to wrest it again from their control. When the pious commanders and all the Christ-loving army had assembled, they first took counsel, and called upon [our] most compassionate God and His all-pure Mother the all-holy Theotokos, to aid them in their venture. And they commanded the whole army, and the Orthodox people who were with them, to keep a three-day fast, and only then to approach the city. While the Russian army was fasting, our good God, the Lover of mankind, seeing the conversion of His repentant people, quickly showed forth His lovingkindness. In those days, a vision was vouchsafed within the royal city of Moscow, to a certain Greek archbishop of the city of Elasson, by the name of Arsenius, who was being forcibly held by the impious Poles in the fortress within the city. He had been deprived of his home and utterly stripped of his possessions by them; when he had become so weak through starvation that he was at his last gasp, suddenly the venerable Sergius of Radonezh, the wonderworker, appeared to him.

"The Archbishop heard someone approach the door of his cell and softly repeat the customary prayer; suddenly, this visitor entered his cell, and a great light shone forth. Then he was told: 'Arsenius, behold! the Lord God hath hearkened unto the supplication of His servants, and for the sake of the entreaties of His immaculate Mother, our all-holy Mistress, the Theotokos and ever-virgin Mary, and of the great wonderworkers Peter, Alexis and Jonah. And with them I also was a mediator [for you]. In the morning, the Lord God will give this city into the hands of the Orthodox Christians, and will cast down your enemies!' The Archbishop lifted up his eyes and beheld the venerable Sergius standing near his bed. Though he could barely move because of his great pain, he rose from his bed and bowed down before him. But the venerable one vanished, and the great light which filled his cell straightway dissipated. When the Archbishop recovered from this awesome vision, he sensed that the great pain which had afflicted him had departed and that his health had returned.

"News of this vision soon reached the ears of the pious military commanders and all the Orthodox Russian forces. And straightway, heartened by the words of Saint Sergius, they arrayed themselves for battle and marched upon the city; soon Kitai Gorod fell to them, on October 22nd, 1612. And they hemmed the impious Poles inside the Kremlin. Perceiving that there was no escape from the Russian army, they quickly surrendered, and opened the Kremlin to them. On Sunday, the pious commanders assembled, and with them archimandrites, and priests from the clergy, and all the Christ-loving forces, and, taking up the precious cross and the holy icons, they proceeded to the Lobnoe Mesto [an elevated platform in Red Square from which formal proclamations were made] and there celebrated services of thanksgiving. And from the Kremlin there came forth to meet them the above-mentioned Archbishop Arsenius of Elasson, and with him a number of the clergy who before had been held in the citadel, bearing with them the icon of the all-holy Theotokos of Vladimir, and precious crosses, and other holy icons.

"When the pious commanders and all the Christ-loving army beheld that icon of the Mother of God, which they had never hoped to see again, they kissed it, shedding a multitude of tears in their joy. And they entered into the Kremlin and celebrated the usual procession. And thus they came to the great Cathedral Church of the Dormition of the All-holy Theotokos. Having celebrated the Liturgy, they gave praise to the Lord in great joy and gladness. Then they dispersed, each to his own home, glorifying and giving thanks unto God and the all-holy Theotokos. And ever since, a feast of the all-holy Theotokos has been appointed for the 22nd of October, the day on which a most glorious victory was won through the supplications of the Mother of God; and it remains as a memorial to future generations, unto the glory of Christ God, to Whom be glory, now and ever, and unto the ages of ages. Amen. " (Prolog, Vol. I, pp. 185b-187a [Moscow: Synodal Press?, 1802]).

In commemoration of the wondrous assistance of the Mistress of heaven, Tsar Michael Feodorovich, who was elected to the throne in the same year, 1612, established, with the blessing of his father, Metropolitan Philaret, annual feasts in honor of the Kazan' icon to be celebrated twice a year: on July 8th, the day of the icon's discovery, and on October 22nd, the day of the liberation of Moscow from the Poles. Furthermore, there were organized in Moscow two processions, from the Cathedral of the Dormition to the Church of the Entrance into the Temple, where Prince Pozharsky had first enshrined his copy of the miraculous Kazan' icon and adorned it with many precious stones. But in 1649, Tsar Alexis Mikhailovich proclaimed that the October 22nd feast would be celebrated throughout the realm.

At Great Vespers

We chant "Blessed is the man...", the first antiphon

*At "Lord, I have cried...," eight stichera: four in Tone IV:
Spec. Mel: "As one valiant among the martyrs..."—*

As the all-beauteous palace of the Word* and His light-bearing throne, O Mistress,* thou didst contain within thy womb* the Word Who is equally enthroned with the Father.* And having given birth unto the never-waning Light, thou hast brought light to our darkness,* hast driven away the falsehood of the serpent and destroyed corruption,* and by thy birthgiving hast granted everlasting life to the world.* Thou hast opened the gates of paradise and bestowed all manner of blessings upon human nature.* And now, do thou by thy supplications, O Lady, deliver thy servants from all misfortunes.

As thou art the great Queen* and Mother of the King of the all-exalted hosts in heaven,* stretching forth thine all-pure hands,* thou dost intercede for us with supplication;* and on earth, as a mighty helper,* thou abidest with thy servants in spirit and in thy divine icon,* and dost gladly save* and deliverest from all temptation* them that piously confess thee to be the Theotokos.

As a paradise of golden radiance,* an all-beauteous palace of divine light,* a holy tree overshadowed by the Holy Spirit,* a habitation of the never-waning Light,* shining manifestly with divine splendor upon them that know thee,* thou dost illumine all creation with thine Infant;* and entreating Him, O Queen and Theotokos,* save all Orthodox hierarchs and people* who flee to thee from all misfortunes.

The Church of God, made splendid* with the icon of thee and thy Son, O Theotokos,* as with royal purple and fine linen,* is adorned with miracles.* Today, at the revelation of thine image, it calleth all to celebrate,*

13

shining with the grace of the Holy Spirit more brightly than the radiance of the sun,* pouring forth streams of healing* upon the sick and the infirm,* and granting rich mercy unto all.

And these stichera, in Tone VIII—

O Jesus, exalted and unapproachable King, Who art enthroned with the Father and the divine Spirit, and Who wast well-pleased to be born on earth of the Virgin who tasted not of wedlock: taking pity on thy creation, bestowing ineffable beauties upon human nature, accept Thou the supplications of Thy Mother which are offered to Thee in our behalf; and be not mindful of our iniquities, but, as Thou art compassionate, remember and save our souls. *Twice*

Bowing down the heavens, the King of glory condescended to restore Adam who had become all corrupt through his transgression; He made His abode within thee, O pure Virgin, was born without violating the seal of thy virginity, and, though King of the archangels, was borne in thine arms, a lowly Babe. And now He accepteth thine entreaty, and fulfilleth thy petition in all things, in that He is thy Son and God. Therefore, beseech Him earnestly, that He save our souls, in that He is compassionate.

More than the tabernacle of Moses, which was fashioned according to a heavenly plan, did God hallow thee wholly with the Holy Spirit, O Theotokos; and, having dwelt wholly within thee, He hath given life to all men. Wherefore, thine icon also hath been filled with the grace of God more than the ark of Aaron, and poureth forth sanctification upon souls and bodies. And bowing down with love before it, we ask of thee great mercy, that thou save our souls, O blessed helper.

Glory..., Now and ever..., in Tone VIII—

Come, let us rejoice in the mighty helper of our race, the Queen and Theotokos! Come, let us bow down before her serene, wondrous and precious image, which is venerated by the angels! For the Theotokos giveth abundant gifts of healing to the faithful, pouring forth never-failing grace from the inexhaustible wellspring of her holy icon. She delivereth from the darkness of temptations and misfortunes, and from every sin, us who piously and in God-pleasing manner glorify and honor the radiant and wondrous holy icon of the Mother of God. Wherefore, chanting, we cry aloud to the prototype thereof: Rejoice, O loving help of the world, in the salvation of our souls!

Entrance.
Prokimenon of the Day.
And three lessons:

READING FROM THE FIRST BOOK OF MOSES,
CALLED GENESIS (28:10-17).

And Jacob went out from Beersheba, and went toward Haran. And he lighted upon a certain place, and tarried there all night, because the sun was set; and he took of the stones of that place, and put them for his pillows, and lay down in that place to sleep. And he dreamed, and behold a ladder set up on the earth, and the top of it reached to heaven: and behold the angels of God ascending and descending on it. And, behold, the Lord stood above it, and said, I am the Lord God of Abraham thy father, and the God of Isaac: the land whereon thou liest, to thee will I give it, and to thy seed; and thy seed shall be as the dust of the earth; and thou shalt be spread abroad to the west, and to the east, and to the north, and to the south: and in thee and in thy seed shall all the families of the earth be blessed. And, behold, I am with thee, and will keep thee in all places whither thou goest, and will bring thee again into this land; for I will not leave thee, until I have done that which I have spoken to thee of. And Jacob awakened out of his sleep, and he said, Surely the Lord is in this place; and I knew it not. And he was afraid, and said, How dreadful is this place! this is none other but the house of God, and this is the gate of heaven.

And when these days are expired, it shall be, that upon the eighth day, and so forward, the priests shall make your burnt offerings upon the altar, and your peace offerings: and I will accept you, saith the Lord God. Then he brought me back the way of the gate of the outward sanctuary which looketh toward the east; and it was shut. Then said the Lord unto me; This gate shall be shut, it shall not be opened, and no man shall enter in by it; because the Lord the God of Israel hath entered in by it, therefore it shall be shut. It is for the prince; the prince, he shall sit in it to eat bread before the Lord; he shall enter by the way of the porch of that gate, and shall go out by the way of the same. Then brought he me the way of the north gate before the house: and I looked, and, behold, the glory of the Lord filled the house of the Lord: and I fell upon my face.

READING FROM THE PROVERBS (9:1-11).

Wisdom hath builded her house, she hath hewn out her seven pillars: she hath killed her beasts; she hath mingled her wine; she hath also furnished her table. She hath sent forth her maidens: she crieth upon the highest places of the city, Whoso is simple, let him turn in hither: as for him that wanteth understanding, she saith to him, Come, eat of my bread, and drink of the wine which I have mingled. Forsake the foolish, and live; and go in the way of understanding. He that reproveth a scorner getteth to himself shame: and he that rebuketh a wicked man getteth himself a blot. Reprove not a scorner, lest he hate thee: rebuke a wise man, and he will love thee. Give instruction to a wise man, and he will be yet wiser: teach a just man, and he will increase in learning. The fear of the Lord is the beginning of wisdom: and the knowledge of the Holy is understanding. For by me thy days shall be multiplied, and the years of thy life shall be increased.

At the Litia, these stichera, in Tone II: Idiomela—

As thine icon, O Theotokos, is truly more venerable than the ark of old before which David danced, having assembled the ranks of Israel, there now stand before it the councils of hierarchs with the ranks of the angels, kings and princes, and all the multitude of the Christian people; and they bless thee, the Mother of God; they glorify thee as befitteth servants, and honor and bow down before thee; and they pray to thee, after God, that thou grant the world peace in Orthodoxy, make steadfast the scepters of kings, and save thy servants from all evils, in that thou art blessed.

Before thine image, O all-pure Lady Theotokos, stand the company of hierarchs, kings and princes, and all the people, monastics and laity, who know thee truly to be a powerful and invincible helper; and they are moved to offer thee supplications with all their soul, and are impelled to pray to God, needful of thine aid, that thou mightest stretch forth thy God-bearing hands and pray for the world. Hearken thou and give ear, O Mistress, and grant consolation to thy servants, lest our heavy and grievous sins gain the victory over us; for we are all ever in need of thine assistance.

In Tone VIII— When first thine icon was painted by Luke, the Evangelist of the mysteries of the Gospel, and was brought to thee, O Queen, that thou mightest make it thine own and impart to it the power to save them that honor thee, thou didst rejoice; and as thou art the merciful collaborator in our salvation, in that once thou didst conceive God in thy womb, thou didst chant a hymn to the icon, giving mouth and voice thereto: "Behold, from henceforth all generations shall call me blessed!", and, gazing at it thou didst say with authority: "My grace and power are with this image!" And we truly believe what thou didst say, O Lady, for in this image thou art with us. Wherefore, standing reverently before it, we thy servants bow down before thee. Visit us with thy maternal compassion.

In Tone VII— A great and all-glorious mountain art thou, O Theotokos, surpassing Mount Sinai. For, unable to bear the descent of the glory of God in types and shadows, it caught on fire, and thunder and lightning struck it; but thou, being all divine light, bore the Word of God in thy womb without being consumed, and with the milk of thy breasts didst nurture Him Who holdeth all things in His hand. And now, as thou dost possess maternal boldness toward Him, O Mistress, help them that faithfully celebrate thine honored festival, and visiting us in thy mercy, forget us not; for thou hast received from God the gift of ordering and protecting the Christian flock, thy servants.

Glory..., Now and ever..., in Tone VI—

To thee do all the generations of men offer gifts of praise, and they entreat thee as Queen and the Mother of God: the prophets proclaimed thee most wisely, the Levites blessed thee, the apostles and martyrs confessed thee, kings and princes bow down before thee, hierarchs proclaim thee, monks and layfolk render thee reverence, rich and poor, orphans and widows, and men of every age and station, old and young, flee beneath thy mighty protection with faith. By thy prayers, O Lady, protect and preserve us, and save our souls from misfortunes.

At the Aposticha, these stichera, in Tone VIII—

O Theotokos, thou honored habitation of the all-pure Light, how can we, thy slaves, worthily hymn thee? For by the revelation of the all-pure icon of thee and the preeternal Infant are all sanctified.

Stichos: I shall commemorate thy name in every generation and generation.

O undefiled Virgin, full of divine joy, what thanks can we ever offer unto thee? For by the most radiant effulgence of thy blessed birthgiving thou hast led all up from corruption to life.

Stichos: Hearken, O daughter, and see, and incline thine ear.

O Virgin Lady, Mother of the Creator, joy of the ranks of heaven and blessed helper of the human race: pray for the salvation of our souls.

Glory..., Now and ever..., in Tone V—

O ye people, let us splendidly chant the hymn of David to the Maiden Bride of God, the Mother of Christ the King: At Thy right hand stood the Queen, O Master, arrayed in a vesture of inwoven gold and adorned with divine splendors. Making her more beautiful than all the world, in that she is good and elect among women, Thou wast well-pleased to be born of her in Thy great mercy, and hast given her as a helper to Thy people, to save and protect them from misfortunes by Thine omnipotent and divine power. By her supplications, O Christ God, have mercy upon us.

Troparion, in Tone IV—

O earnest helper, Mother of the Lord Most High, thou dost entreat Christ, thy Son and our God, in behalf of all, and causest all to be saved who have recourse to thy mighty protection. O Lady, Queen and Mistress, help us all who, amid temptations, sorrows and sickness, are heavy laden with many sins, who stand before thee and with tears pray to thee with compunctionate soul and contrite heart before thine all-pure image, and who have unfailing hope in thee: grant deliverance from all evils, and things profitable unto all, O Virgin Theotokos, and save us all, for thou art the divine protection of thy servants.

At Matins

At "God is the Lord...," the troparion of the icon, thrice.

After the first chanting of the Psalter, this Sedalen, in Tone III—

O pious people, ye assemblies of Orthodox Christians, draw ye all nigh with faith, falling down before the divine image of the Mother. of God; for she joyfully granteth healing to all the ailing, woundeth the heretical like a shaft from a bow, maketh us all radiantly glad, and illumineth us with grace by her supplications.

Glory..., Now and ever...—

God made thee wholly a good and undefiled Virgin among women, having prefigured thee honorably through the prophets; and having blessed thee by His priests, He caused thee to dwell in the Holy of Holies and nurtured thee by an angel, giving thee bread from heaven. And the same all-good One, the only-begotten Word of God, made His abode within thee and issued forth from thee in the flesh. Wherefore, we worship and honor thee truly as the true Theotokos.

After the second chanting of the Psalter, this Sedalen, in Tone IV—

Let all the multitude of the faithful radiantly join chorus, and let the army of the demons lament, beholding the manifold feasts of the Mother of God shining forth, praising the blessed Mother of God with divine hymns. For where the all-blessed Mistress Theotokos, the divinely elect Maiden, is glorified in God-pleasing manner, there are the fall of wickedness and the mighty confirmation of Christians.

Glory..., Now and ever...—

O most blessed Mistress Theotokos, divinely elect Maiden, splendid fulfillment of the words of the prophets, boast of the apostles, crown and confession of the martyrs, greatly hymned one who art honored by the angels and the generations of men, longed-for helper of the whole world: deliver thy servants from future damnation and the lake of fire, O thou who alone art blessed.

After the Polyeleos, this Sedalen, in Tone I—

O Mother of God, save them that honor thee in Orthodox manner, and flee to thee, and lovingly bow down before thy holy icon; and give us not as plunder to our adversaries, neither let all the evils which our sins have prepared for us come upon us, nor let our iniquities gain ascendancy over our heads; but may thy God-pleasing maternal prayers to God win the victory.

Glory..., Now and ever...—

Thine all-pure icon, O Virgin Theotokos, is spiritual healing for the whole world; and having recourse thereto, we bow down before thee, and venerate, kiss and honor it, drawing forth therefrom the grace of healing of bodily infirmities and the passions of the spirit; and thus are we freed by thy supplications.

Song of Ascents, the first antiphon of Tone IV.

Prokimenon, in Tone IV—
I shall commemorate thy name in every generation and generation.
Stichos: Hearken, O daughter, and see, and incline thine ear.

"Let every breath praise the Lord..."

GOSPEL ACCORDING TO LUKE, §4 [LK 1:39-49, 56]
And Mary arose in those days, and went into the hill country with haste, into a city of Judah; and entered into the house of Zechariah, and saluted Elisabeth. And it came to pass, that, when Elisabeth heard the salutation of Mary, the babe leaped in her womb; and Elisabeth was

filled with the Holy Ghost: and she spake out with a loud voice, and said, Blessed art thou among women, and blessed is the fruit of thy womb. And whence is this to me, that the mother of my Lord should come to me? For, lo, as soon as the voice of thy salutation sounded in mine ears, the babe leaped in my womb for joy. And blessed is she that believed: for there shall be a performance of those things which were told her from the Lord. And Mary said, My soul doth magnify the Lord, and my spirit hath rejoiced in God my Savior. For He hath regarded the low estate of His handmaiden: for, behold, from henceforth all generations shall call me blessed. For He that is mighty hath done to me great things; and holy is His name. And Mary abode with her about three months, and returned to her own house.

After Psalm 50, this sticheron, in Tone VIII—
Come, let us rejoice in the mighty helper of our race, the Queen and Theotokos! Come, let us bow down before her serene, wondrous and precious image, which is venerated by the angels! For the Theotokos giveth abundant gifts of healing to the faithful, pouring forth never-failing grace from the inexhaustible well-spring of her holy icon. She delivereth from the darkness of temptations and misfortunes, and from every sin, us who piously and in God-pleasing manner glorify and honor the radiant and wondrous holy icon of the Mother of God. Wherefore, chanting, we cry aloud to the prototype thereof: Rejoice, O loving help of the world, in the salvation of our souls!

Ode I
Canon to the Directress, the all-holy Theotokos, with six troparia, including the Irmos, the composition of the priest-monk Ignatius, in Tone IV—
Irmos: I shall open my lips, and with the Spirit shall they be filled; and I shall utter discourse unto the Queen Mother, and shall appear radiantly keeping festival, and rejoicing I shall hymn her wonders.

22

O pure one, joyously do I now offer my foremost praise: Rejoice! And with gladsome voice I cry out to thee, O Directress: Rejoice, and fill me with understanding as I begin to hymn thee!

Rejoice, O all-hymned one who gavest birth unto Christ our everlasting Joy! O Directress, thou hope of the Orthodox, all-hymned Virgin, fill me with the joy which the world hath desired.

All men and angels join chorus, ever crying out together in heaven and on earth, O Directress: Rejoice, O Virgin, for by thy birthgiving thou hast filled all things with joy!

O Directress, vouchsafe joy unto them that with fear cry out to thee Rejoice!, in that thou art the Mother of joy who deliverest from all tribulations; and have mercy on all that have recourse to thee.

Another canon of the feast, with eight troparia, in the same tone—
Irmos: (same as that of the preceding canon)

The leaders of the angels reverence thee, O Theotokos; and the ranks of the saints serve thee with honor; the righteous adorn themselves and bless thee as the mediatress of heavenly things; heaven and earth together praise thee splendidly in gladness. And we sinners ask mercy: Illumine our hearts, O Mistress, that we may chant a hymn to the revelation of thy holy icon.

Come ye, O Christian people, having mystically cleansed your minds, and assemble in the holy church of the Mother of Christ our God; for from her holy icon there poureth forth upon us inexhaustibly a spiritual wellspring which healeth the souls and bodies of them that cry out in song: Blessed is our God Who was born of thee!

The strange wonder of thy divine birthgiving striketh every ear with wonder and awe, O all-immaculate one: how thou didst conceive the Creator of the cherubim; how thou didst bear in the flesh Him Who is life and for the whole world didst give birth to life: the God and Man!

Beneath thy shelter do all we, the generations of man, flee, O Virgin Lady. With the light of thy birthgiving enlighten us, thy sinful servants who earnestly pray, bowing down before thine all-pure icon, asking to receive from thee great mercy.

Katavasia: I shall open my lips...

Ode III
First Canon

Irmos: O Theotokos, thou living and abundant fountain, in thy divine glory establish thou them that hymn thee and that spiritually form themselves into a choir; and vouchsafe unto them crowns of glory.

Rejoice, O unshakable, pure and animate palace of Christ the King Most High! Rejoice, O Directress, Rejoice! For by thee is our city preserved intact!

In thy womb which tasted not of wedlock thou didst bodily contain Him Creation cannot contain, O Virgin Directress. Wherefore, magnifying thee as is meet, we chant Rejoice!

O all-hymned joy of the world, ever hymning thee with joy, O pure one, we are vouchsafed everlasting joy by thy maternal supplications unto Him Who was born of thee, O Directress.

O Directress, we invoke thee as the golden jar, the candlestick, the rod and the table, O pure one, and we ever raise the cry Rejoice! to thee when we use these terms.

Second Canon
Irmos: (same as that of the preceding canon)

What worthy praise can our utter infirmity offer thee? For through the manifestation of thine all-pure, divine icon thou pourest forth bountiful streams of healing upon thy servants who faithfully have recourse to thee.

The holy revelation of thy divine icon, O Virgin Theotokos, hath shone upon us like the radiant sun, emitting rays of all-glorious miracles, and dispelling a myriad of evil circumstances by thy sacred intercessions, O Mistress.

24

Thou didst once fill thy first-painted icon with grace, O Virgin Lady Theotokos; and now that same grace speaketh forth truly in the effulgence of the wonders of faith, as the first one did for the sake of thee who wast first depicted thereon, unto them that with faith have recourse to thee after God.

We bow down before the all-pure image of thee and thy Babe all-sweet, Christ the pre-eternal and never-waning Light, O Theotokos, by Whom thou hast saved all human nature from cruel evils and mortal corruption.

Sedalen, in Tone VIII: Spec. Mel.: "Of the Wisdom..."—

The divine apostles of the Word, the clarion-voiced universal heralds of the Gospel of Christ, having founded a divine church in thine all-holy name, O Theotokos, approached thee, entreating thee to come to its consecration. But thou didst say, O Mother of God: "Go in peace, and I shall be with you there!" And they, going forth, found there, on the wall of the church, the likeness of thine image limned powerfully in colored hues; and seeing it, they did thee homage and glorified God. And we also, with them, bow down before thy divine icon, asking of thee great mercy. Grant thou remission of sins to thy servants, O thou who alone art blessed.

Glory..., Now and ever...: the above Sedalen is repeated.

ODE IV
First Canon

Irmos: Seated in glory upon the throne of the Godhead, Jesus most divine is come upon a light cloud, and with His incorrupt arm He hath saved them that cry: Glory to Thy power, O Christ!

Rejoice, O Mistress Directress, thou wonder of wonders! Rejoice, joy of all cities and towns, impregnable fortress and bulwark for Christians amid misfortunes, thou victory over the enemy!

Rejoice, rejoice, O boast of Orthodox kings, for thou, O Queen of all, dost accompany Christ-loving armies! Rejoice, O Directress, thou refuge and confirmation of us all!

Rejoice, deliverance for all amid misfortunes! Rejoice, ready consolation for all the sorrowful! Rejoice, O all-hymned one! Rejoice, most blessed Directress, healer of all the infirm!

Rejoice, thou whose mighty works all creation doth make haste to glorify as is meet; yet it is unable, O Directress, and therefore it crieth out to thee! Rejoice, O Mistress, thou dwelling-place which contained God!

Second Canon
Irmos: (same as that of the preceding canon)

O ye pure people, in purity let us honor the icon of the Virgin Theotokos and of the divine Infant Christ our God; and let us kiss it and glorify her with fear and trembling; for we right honorably venerate the icon and honor even more the pure Mother of God.

David, the divine and wondrous prophet, foreseeing as from a great distance, said: The rich among the people shall entreat thy countenance. And let us, O ye faithful, bow down and venerate the precious icon, sanctified body and soul.

Luke, the divinely eloquent recorder of the Gospel, at the behest of God set down thine all-immaculate image, O Theotokos, depicting the pre-eternal Infant in thine arms; and from temptations and misfortunes thou deliverest them that have recourse thereto, and thou protectest and savest them all by thine image.

Thou art the boast and crown of all the saints, O Queen; after God, thou art our hope and helper, and on thee have we all set our hope of salvation. Thee do we entreat as the Mother of God: Rain down thy rich and soul-saving mercies upon thy sinful servants.

First Canon

Irmos: All things are filled with awe at thy divine glory, for thou, O Virgin who hast not known wedlock, didst have within thy womb Him Who is God over all, and didst give birth to the timeless Son, granting peace unto all that hymn thee.

Thou art an abyss of goodness and compassions. Rejoice, O Virgin Directress! Rejoice, thou who makest all faithful! O rejoice, most speedy helper of them that are in misfortune and sorrow!

Beholding the mighty works of the fullness of thy wonders, we, the faithful, are filled with joy; and they among us who hear of them see them not. Wherefore, in every place we all ever chant unto thee, Rejoice, O Directress!

O rejoice, O Virgin Directress, thou dwelling-place of Christ our God and habitation of His ineffable and all-divine glory! O rejoice, palace all adorned! Rejoice, animate city ever reigning!

Looking upon thee as a sea of joy inexhaustible, O Virgin Maiden Directress, rejoicing we all cry out to thee: Rejoice! And chanting, we ever expect of thee divine gifts invisibly bestowed.

Second Canon

Irmos: (same as that of the preceding canon)

Every being is at a loss how to hymn thee, O all-pure one; for thou art exalted far above the heavenly intelligences, having given birth unto the unapproachable and dread King and God of all. But as thou art merciful and the ready helper of men, attend unto the entreaty of thy servants, and grant us thy help.

Where thy grace overshadoweth, O Theotokos, the demons vanish in fear and their wickedly devised phantasy is destroyed; the dark demons flee and the whole multitude of the faithful rejoice, crying out a hymn of praise to thee from their hearts: Rejoice, thou divine protection of our souls!

Sweet sight is given to the eyeless, hearing to the deaf, good speech to the mute, the ability to walk to the lame, cleansing to the leprous, chastity to the demonized, and healing to them that suffer from divers sicknesses, through the overshadowing of thine all-pure icon, O Theotokos.

O joyous Theotokos, let us never fail to hymn thy mighty works with psalms and hymns; for thou truly gavest birth unto the incarnate God unto our universal salvation and deliverance.

Ode VI
First Canon

Irmos: Celebrating this divine and most honored festival of the Mother of God, come, ye divinely wise, let us clap our hands and glorify God Who was born of her!

Receiving Christ within thyself, O pure Virgin Directress, thou didst hear the cry: Rejoice! And having given birth unto Him ineffably, thou dost ever hear the salutation Rejoice! from all.

Thou hast filled all with joy, and hast united them that are on high with them below, O Directress. Wherefore, with joy heaven and all the earth now cry out to thee together.

Rejoice, O all-hymned Directress, consolation of widows and all orphans! Rejoice, thou that pourest forth inexhaustible riches upon all the destitute!

Rejoice, O Directress, dwelling-place of Christ, more lustrous than any gold and more splendid than the dawning of the sun! Rejoice, O Virgin! Rejoice, O Bride unwedded!

Second Canon
Irmos: (same as that of the preceding canon)

O Virgin Lady, of old thou didst by thine exclamation impart to thine all-pure image the all-rich grace of thy

28

divine birthgiving, that it work great and all-glorious miracles in abundance, unto the salvation of them that set their hope on thee.

Where the holy name of the joyous Theotokos is glorified, streams of every good thing pour forth. Come ye in purity, O people, for, lo! by the manifestation of the divine icon of the Virgin is the presence of the Queen revealed, unto the salvation of all the faithful.

Approaching with faith, O all-immaculate Mistress and Mother of God, from thine all-pure icon we receive healing of maladies, the dispelling of the passions, salvation which nourisheth the soul, forgiveness of sins, and everlasting deliverance.

To thee, O Lady, do the generations of the earthborn flee, and ask great mercy; and they that are infirm receive healing in abundance, release from the passions, and consolation amid grief. O Mistress, let fall upon me a drop of soul-saving rain, that with all I also may hymn thy magnitude.

Kontakion, in Tone VIII: Spec. Mel." To thee, the champion leader..."—

O ye people, let us flee to that calm and good haven, the speedy helper and ready and fervent salvation, the protection of the Virgin, and let us make haste to prayer and speed to repentance. For the all-pure Theotokos poureth forth upon us inexhaustible mercies; she goeth before to help us and delivereth her good-hearted and God-fearing servants from great misfortunes and evils.

Ikos: Having cleansed thought and mind, let us make haste to the Theotokos, calling her blessed in splendid hymns; and let us glorify and honor her all-pure icon, and falling down before it, let us do homage as to herself; for the veneration shown an icon ascendeth unto the Prototype, and he that honoreth and boweth down before it, honoreth the Prototype Himself, as the divine fathers have said. And if one doth not reverence the all-holy Theotokos, and doth not venerate her icon, let him be anathema. For she putteth to shame and destroyeth them that honor her not, and delivereth from great misfortunes and evils her good-hearted and God-fearing servants.

ODE VII
First Canon

Irmos: The divinely wise youths worshipped not a creation rather than the Creator, but, manfully trampling the threat of the fire underfoot, they rejoiced, chanting: Blessed art Thou, the all-hymned Lord and God of our fathers!

Rejoice, rejoice, O Directress, who dost ever direct all the faithful to tread the path to all salvation! Rejoice, O Mistress, for by thee are we ever delivered from the present tribulations brought about by the barbarians!

Rejoice, rejoice, O Theotokos Directress, who keepest watch and prayest to God for us, delivering all the people from every sorrow and from all evil by thy mediation!

Rejoice, rejoice, O all-holy Directress, who fulfillest those of our petitions which are for our profit, and ever desirest for all good and brotherly unity, especially among the leaders.

Rejoice, rejoice, O Directress of ships which must needs sail, who deliverest the faithful, and quickly loosest them from divers and long-standing ailments, O deliverance of all from every sorrow!

Second Canon
Irmos: (same as that of the preceding canon)

Come ye, let us draw forth remission from the inexhaustible well-spring which poureth forth sanctity, the all-pure Virgin and her all-pure Infant, God the Word, Who becameth incarnate for our sake. And let us cry out to Him: O Creator and Deliverer Who art God glorified with the Father and the Spirit, blessed art Thou!

Possessed of ever-vigilant and God-pleasing prayer, O pure one, and an insuperable dominion of might, crush thou the audacity of the enemy which is directed against us, that we, thy servants, may rejoice in thee, crying out to thy Son: O God of our fathers, blessed art Thou!

O ye faithful people, let us rejoice and be glad in the wondrous appearance of the icon of the all-pure Mistress, the Theotokos; for it hath been shown to be an inexhaustible river pouring forth the water of healing. For it giveth sight to the blind, hearing to the deaf, the ability to walk to the lame, and free healing to all amid their infirmities.

An unfathomable abyss, an incomprehensible mystery is the unapproachable image of thy conception, O Virgin; for thy conception was seedless; thou gavest birth without a husband; the Incorporeal One becameth incarnate, the Pre-eternal One becameth an infant, the Son of God becameth thy Son, O Virgin. To Him do we cry aloud: Blessed art Thou, O God!

Ode VIII
First Canon

Irmos: The Offspring of the Theotokos saved the pious youths in the furnace: then in figure, but now in deed; and she moveth all the world to chant to Thee: Hymn the Lord, ye works, and exalt Him supremely for all ages!

Rejoice, O most blessed Mary, for through thee the most blessed God hath arrayed Himself in all of me; and having arrayed Himself in man, He hath united man to His divinity in an ineffable union, O Virgin Directress! Rejoice, O joyous one, thou joy of all the world!

Rejoice, dispeller of evil spirits! Rejoice, O Theotokos Directress! Rejoice, thou whom the invisible armies of heaven ever glorify and magnify as the Mother of God! Rejoice, thou who hast joined them that are below with them above!

Rejoice, rejoice, O Directress who without exception surpassest all the heavenly hosts! Rejoice, O all-hymned Mistress, who gavest birth to the God of all creation, and hast dominion over it! Rejoice, O pure one, who even after giving birth remainest a virgin!

Rejoice, glory of all women, all-hallowed temple of our God! Rejoice, O Directress! Rejoice, thou who savest the souls of all the world! Rejoice, protecting cloud broader than the heavens! Rejoice, phial full of divine oil of myrrh!

Second Canon
Irmos: (same as that of the preceding canon)

The minds of angels and men are filled with awe, O Theotokos, at how thou gavest flesh unto the God of heaven, containing Him in thy womb, and how, having given birth unto Him as a babe, thou bearest Him as a Son in thine arms. Before Him doth creation stand in awe and the heavenly thrones tremble, crying out unceasingly: Holy, holy, holy art Thou, O God Who art all-hymned and supremely exalted above all forever!

Rejoice, thou who art the joy of all the world! With the Archangel Gabriel we cry out to thee, O Theotokos: Rejoice, thou who didst contain the Infinite One! Rejoice, O thou who art full of grace, bearer of the whole Divinity! Rejoice, restoration of Adam, the Lord is with thee, saving us for thy sake! Him do we hymn and exalt supremely forever.

O sanctified root of Jesse, thou hast plucked forth the root of our sin, O rod of Aaron which blossomed, giving rise to a Blossom, Christ the Bestower of life! O jar which received the Manna, thou hast crushed all the power of death, and hast brought the human race to the generation of life. Wherefore, we hymn thee, the cause of that which is good.

Thou art the boast of Christians, O Mistress; thou art a sword against our enemies and a rampart for them that have recourse unto thee. We now call upon thee for aid, O Lady: permit not the foe to rise up against thy people, for they praise neither thee nor thy Son, O Theotokos, nor do they bow down before thine icon. Vanquish them, and save thou our souls.

First Canon

Irmos: Let every earthborn man leap for joy, enlightened by the Spirit, and let the nature of the incorporeal intelligences keep festival, honoring the sacred feast of the Mother of God, and let them cry aloud: Rejoice, O most blessed Theotokos, pure Ever-virgin!

Rejoice, O lamp who bore the never-waning Light and who in thy birth-giving hast destroyed the darkness of polytheism and delivered thy people from the abyss of hades! Rejoice, O Theotokos Directress, mediatress of all good things!

Rejoice, O earth from whence the Ear of heavenly grain hath budded forth for the faithful; and deliver the whole world from soul-destroying famine, O noetic and animate one! Rejoice, O vine who gavest birth to the Cluster of life, O pure Theotokos Directress!

Rejoice, most comely paradise of mystic flowers! Rejoice, Virgin Mother, O Theotokos who by purity hast most strangely vanquished the understanding of the invisible foe! Rejoice, O Maiden, rejoice, O Directress, thou universal wonder and report!

By thine aid, keep thou the remaining time of our life untouched by harm, O Virgin Maiden, and count us worthy of receiving a good end, for we hymn thee and cry aloud: Rejoice, O most blessed and pure Theotokos and Directress!

Second Canon

Irmos: (same as that of the preceding canon)

Thee, the steadfast helper of the human race, O Theotokos Mary, did the choir of the prophets foretell in many and divers ways, as the holy tabernacle more spacious than the heavens, the tablet divinely inscribed, the bush unconsumed by the Fire, the portal through which God passeth, the mountain and the ladder, the bridge and the rod which blossomed forth. And we truly magnify thee as the Theotokos.

The mystery of the depth of thy birthgiving moveth the mind of the angels to awe, O Virgin, and thine all-pure icon driveth the demons away, darkeneth the countenances of the ungodly, and putteth them to shame. For they cannot bear to look upon its power, and they flee and vanish away. And we lovingly bow down and venerate it, and magnify thee as the Theotokos.

As a constant intercessor before the King Most High, in that thou art possessed of undaunted boldness, establish thou the life of the Orthodox in profound peace, exalt our right-believing hierarchs, and ever grant unto thy servants all things profitable, that we may magnify thee as the Theotokos.

O most merciful helper of Christians, the mind of men or angels cannot hymn thee as is meet, for thou art more honorable than all creation, more glorious than all things of heaven and earth; for thou gavest birth unto the Creator and God of all. O Mistress, mercifully accept the hymn which we have composed for thee from the depths of our heart, and ever save us, for on thee have we set our hope.

Exapostilarion—

Let the all-hymned Mother of God be honored, who gaveth birth unto Christ our God, our Life, for she is the opening of the gates of paradise, the cleansing of the whole world, the restoration to life. And He is the One of Whom the prophets spake, and we worship Him as our God, the Savior of our souls. *twice*

Glory..., Now and ever... —

Come ye with purity, O ye faithful, and let us exalt the wondrous icon of the all-pure Mother of our God and Christ, the divine Infant Savior. For, having given birth to Him and borne Him in her arms, and possessing boldness before Him, she prayeth unceasingly for us, and bestoweth upon her servants rich mercies.

34

Let us glorify the joyous Theotokos, O ye faithful, for we ever have her holy and blessed name upon our lips more than any other, unceasingly fleeing to her all-pure and healing icon; for thereby do we find all things good and profitable on earth, and we are delivered from the snares of the demons in the air. Yea, as the Mother who gaveth birth to the Creator of all, she saveth our souls from misfortunes. *twice*

Everlastingly may the assembly of the impious lament, who do not confess thee to be the Theotokos pure in thy birthgiving, and do not bow down before thine all-pure icon. But we, thy faithful people, rejoicing confess thee to be the true Theotokos and Virgin, in that thou didst truly give birth unto Christ our God in the flesh, hast trampled the corruption of Adam underfoot, hast cleansed the whole world of sin, hast granted never-ending life and opened the gates of paradise to the faithful through thy divine Offspring. Him do thou entreat, that we who hymn thy mystery with faith may be saved.

Let all the multitude of the pious be glad and rejoice with ineffable joy; and, falling down, let them all do homage and reverence the Mother of God with fear, giving thanks to her after God, in that she is the mediatress of such great blessings. The angels desire to gaze upon those things which Christ our God hath given to the faithful through the Theotokos, for He hath an abundance of compassions and great and all-rich mercy.

Glory..., Now and ever..., in Tone VIII—

Thy holy icon which depicteth thy form, O Virgin Theotokos, is by thy grace an all-bounteous fountain which poureth forth its waters for all the earth and enlighteneth the whole world with the effulgent radiance of the Holy Spirit. For thou didst ineffably give birth in the flesh to God the Word, hearing such things as these from the Archangel Gabriel: Rejoice, O thou who art full of grace, the Lord is with thee, and the Holy Spirit overshadoweth thee at thy conceiving! And thus didst thou say to the first icon depicting thee, when thou didst gaze upon it: My grace is with it! And thy word was fulfilled in the power of the icon. Divine grace, transcending every image, voice, power, deed and mind, abiding with it forever, unceasingly worketh signs and wonders, and giveth spiritually profitable healing to all that approach it with faith, through thine unceasing divine, maternal supplications to God.

Great Doxology and Dismissal.

At the Liturgy
On the Beatitudes, eight troparia: four from Ode III of Canon I, and four from Ode VI of Canon II.

Prokimenon, in Tone II, the Song of the Theotokos:
My soul doth magnify the Lord, and my spirit hath rejoiced in God my Savior.
Stichos: For He hath looked upon the lowliness of His handmaiden; for behold, from henceforth all generations shall call me blessed.

EPISTLE TO THE PHILIPPIANS, §240 [PHIL 2:5-11]
Brethren: Let this mind be in you, which was also in Christ Jesus: who, being in the form of God, thought it not robbery to be equal with God: but made Himself of no reputation, and took upon Himself the form of a servant, and was made in the likeness of men: and being found in fashion as a man, He humbled Himself, and became obedient unto death, even the death of the cross. Wherefore God also hath highly exalted Him, and given Him a name which is above every name: that at the name of Jesus every knee should bow, of things in heaven, and things in earth, and things under the earth; and that every tongue should confess that Jesus Christ is Lord, to the glory of God the Father.

Alleluia, in Tone VIII—

Stichos: Hearken, O daughter, and see, and incline thine ear.

Stichos: The rich among the people shall entreat thy countenance.

GOSPEL ACCORDING TO ST. LUKE, §54 [LK 10:38-42; 11:27-28]

Now it came to pass, as they went, that He entered into a certain village; and a certain woman named Martha received him into her house. And she had a sister called Mary, which also sat at Jesus' feet, and heard His word. But Martha was cumbered about much serving, and came to Him, and said, Lord, dost Thou not care that my sister hath left me to serve alone? Bid her therefore that she help me. And Jesus answered and said unto her, Martha, Martha, thou art careful and troubled about many things: but one thing is needful; and Mary hath chosen that good part, which shall not be taken away from her. And it came to pass, as He spoke these things, a certain woman of the company lifted up her voice, and said unto Him, Blessed is the womb that bare Thee, and the paps which Thou hast sucked. But He said, Yea, rather, blessed are they that hear the word of God, and keep it.

Communion verse—

I will take the cup of salvation, and I will call upon the name of the Lord.

Kontakion I

To thee, the Theotokos, the helper of the Christian race who art
the elect of all generations, who coverest the Orthodox of our
land with the protection of thy goodness, do we offer hymns of
thanksgiving for the revelation of thy miraculous icon. And as
thou art greatly merciful unto all that have recourse to thee, help
us in all sorrows and wants, all tribulations and dangers, that we
may cry out to thee: Rejoice, O fervent helper of the Christian
race!

Ikos I

An angel, and a chief among them, was sent to say "Rejoice!" to
the Theotokos when God the Word became incarnate within her
womb; and we sinners, glorifying the manifestation of the icon of
her and of the divine Infant, Christ the Savior, with compunction
cry aloud to her that is full of grace:

Rejoice, divinely chosen Maiden!

Rejoice, Mother of God!

Rejoice, Queen of heaven and earth!

Rejoice, radiant adornment of the Church of heaven and
earth!

Rejoice, thou who art hymned by the seraphim!

Rejoice, splendid fulfillment of the prophecies!

Rejoice, boast of the apostles!

Rejoice, confession of the martyrs!

Rejoice, crown of the venerable!

Rejoice, joy of the righteous!

Rejoice, hope of sinners!

Rejoice, thou who art honored by the angels!

Rejoice, O fervent helper of the Christian race!

Kontakion II

Looking down from the heights of thy heavenly abode, where
thou dwellest in glory with thy Son, upon the sorrow of thy
servants in the newly-enlightened city of Kazan', that because of
the visitation of the wrath of God the Faith of Christ was mocked
by the wicked religion of the Moslems, thou wast well pleased to
reveal thine icon, glorifying it with miracles, that, made steadfast by signs of thy grace, the Christ-loving people might cry out
to God with faith: Alleluia!

The wise maiden, seeking to understand the reason for the thrice-repeated appearance of the Mother of God, made haste to the authorities, relating to them tidings concerning the wondrous manifestation and the dreadful threat; and we, marvelling at the understanding given the maid from on high, reverently cry out to the all-blessed one:

Rejoice, thou who perfectest praise for God through the lips of children!

Rejoice, thou who disclosest the mysteries of God's grace unto the young!

Rejoice, report doubtful to infidels!

Rejoice, manifest boast of the faithful!

Rejoice, lightning which frightenest unbelievers!

Rejoice, thou who illuminest the thoughts of the faithful!

Rejoice, reproof of the wicked faith of the Moslems!

Rejoice, ruination of their pride!

Rejoice, confirmation of the Christian Faith!

Rejoice, sanctification of the veneration of the holy icons!

Rejoice, thou who transformest our sorrow into joy!

Rejoice, thou who dost gladden us with certain hope!

Rejoice, O fervent helper of the Christian race!

KONTAKION III

With the grace of the Mother of God the power of the Most High made the maiden wise and imparted strength unto her for the search for the precious gift of God; and boldly, with faith in the Lord, she set about her labor. And, discovering the treasure of the holy icon of the Mother of God in the ground, she joyfully cried out to God: Alleluia!

IKOS III

Possessed of a compassionate concern for the newly-enlightened people of the city of Kazan', O Mistress, thou didst pour forth torrents of miracles from thine all-precious icon, granting vision to the physical eyes of the blind, and spiritually illumining the benighted with the light of the knowledge of God and piety, according unto all a refuge untouched by storm beneath the virginal overshadowing of thine icon. Wherefore, we cry aloud to thee:

Rejoice, thou who dispellest the darkness of grievous circumstances with the appearance of thine icon!

Rejoice, thou who enlightenest all with the rays of thy wonders!

Rejoice, recovery of the sight of the blind!

Rejoice, enlightenment of the benighted through understanding!

Rejoice, glory of Orthodoxy!

Rejoice, calm haven for them that seek salvation!

Rejoice, Mother of chastity!

Rejoice, protection and safeguarding of virginity!

Rejoice, thou for whose sake all the multitude of the faithful join chorus!

Rejoice, thou for whose sake the horde of the demons is filled with lamentation!

Rejoice, help for which all Christians long!

Rejoice, joy of all that sorrow!

Rejoice, O fervent helper of the Christian race!

KONTAKION IV

The blessed Hermogenes, the recorder of the miracles of thine icon, O Mother of God, endeavoring to quell the tempest of tumults and sedition which was raised in the Russian land by her enemies, shed tears in prayer before it; and seeing that thine icon was given as a shield and a standard of victory to the Orthodox forces, strengthened with faith, until the end of his life he cried out to God: Alleluia!

IKOS IV

The Orthodox soldiers, hearing the mystery revealed by the venerable Sergius to the holy hierarch Arsenius, that, by the intercession of the Mother of God, the judgement of their homeland would be turned to mercy, took up the icon of the Mother of God as a standard of victory, rescued the mother of Russian cities from the hands of the adversary, and cried aloud to the helper of Christians:

Rejoice, Mother of God Most High!

Rejoice, for thou entreatest thy Son, Christ our God, in behalf of all!

Rejoice, for thou dost cause all to be saved who have recourse to thy mighty protection!

Rejoice, helper of all amid sorrow and sickness!

Rejoice, thou who givest those things which are profitable unto all that pray before thine all-pure image with contrite heart!

40

Rejoice, deliverance from evil for all that have unwavering trust in thee!

Rejoice, good and calm haven!

Rejoice, speedy helper!

Rejoice, ready and fervent protection of salvation!

Rejoice, thou who pourest forth inexhaustible mercies upon us!

Rejoice, thou who hastenest beforehand to our aid!

Rejoice, thou who deliverest us from all tribulations!

Rejoice, O fervent helper of the Christian race!

Kontakion V

Thine icon, O Mother of God, hath been shown to be a divinely guided star which hath traversed the whole land of Russia, shining the rays of thy miracles upon all who are lost upon the sea of this life of suffering, driving away the darkness of grief and the gloom of every affliction, and guiding to the path of salvation them that with faith have recourse unto thee and cry out to God: Alleluia!

Ikos V

Tsar Peter, seeing that many wonders were being wrought by God's grace through the holy icon of the Mother of God, took it as a guide for his army and as a shield and protection on the day of battle against the Swedes; and, having utterly vanquished the enemy with the help of the Mother of God, he thus set a perfect stone as a foundation for his new royal city, and thy miraculous icon he placed in the heart of that city as a sanctification, as a shield and wall of defense. Wherefore, we cry out to the all-pure one:

Rejoice, habitation and abode of Christ our God!

Rejoice, place of His ineffable glory!

Rejoice, animate city ever reigning!

Rejoice, palace all-adorned!

Rejoice, joy of cities and villages!

Rejoice, invincible keep and rampart for Christians amid tribulation!

Rejoice, boast of the Orthodox Church!

Rejoice, confirmation of the scepters of kings!

Rejoice, helper of Christ-loving forces!

Rejoice, triumph over the enemy!

Rejoice, deliverance from misfortunes!

Rejoice, thou who visitest all with thy maternal compassions!

Rejoice, O fervent helper of the Christian race!

Standing before thine all-pure image, assemblies of hierarchs, kings, princes and all the people, monks and laymen, have proclaimed thy great mercies, O Lady Theotokos; for thou preservest cities, protectest monastic communities and defendest villages. And knowing thee to be a mighty and invincible helper, they offered up prayers to thee with tears, that thou stretch forth thy God-bearing hands to thy Son for thy people, to deliver all from every misfortune and danger, that we may cry out to God in thanksgiving! Alleluia!

Having shone forth true enlightenment and dispelled the falsehood of Islam in the newly-illumined land, thou didst shine the light of wonders and mercies also in the new royal city; for they that had recourse to thy healing icon with faith received deliverance from sorrows, the healing of infirmities and the fullness of joy, crying out to thee with fervor:

Rejoice, inexhaustible well-spring of sanctity!

Rejoice, river swollen with the grace of God!

Rejoice, reconciliation of sinners with God!

Rejoice, cleansing of our sins!

Rejoice, instructor of piety!

Rejoice, confirmation and help in good works!

Rejoice, thou who acceptest good vows!

Rejoice, thou who aidest good intentions!

Rejoice, thou who dost foil evil undertakings!

Rejoice, thou who settest at nought the wiles of the enemy!

Rejoice, speedy helper of men!

Rejoice, thou who grantest us twofold mercy!

Rejoice, O fervent helper of the Christian race!

When Tsar Alexander the blessed desired to acknowledge the mercies of the all-blessed Queen of heaven and earth, and to offer thanks according to his power for the deliverance of his realm from the incursion of foreigners, to the marvellous church erected in honor of the all-wondrous icon he brought trophies of his victory as a gift, that all, mindful of the mercy of the Mother of God who saved his city and realm, might ever chant unto God with thankful lips: Alleluia!

Ikos VII

Thy holy icon, O Mother of God, was truly shown to the new royal city as a good Directress, like unto the one in Constantinople of old; for the tsars had recourse unto thee, asking thine aid as they set forth on their journeys and began their undertakings; and offering prayers of thanksgiving before thine all-pure icon for deliverance from tribulations and dangers, they acknowledged thee to be a mighty helper and aid. Wherefore, we cry out to thee in thanksgiving:

Rejoice, protection of the land of Russia!

Rejoice, defense and confirmation of Orthodoxy therein!

Rejoice, indestructible shield of the faithful!

Rejoice, impenetrable armor thereof!

Rejoice, thou who layest bare the wiles of the enemy!

Rejoice, thou who rendest them asunder like a spider's web!

Rejoice, reproof of ungodliness!

Rejoice, destruction of sedition!

Rejoice, correction of the young!

Rejoice, consolation of the old!

Rejoice, refutation of teachings harmful to the spirit!

Rejoice, bestowal of knowledge profitable to the soul!

Rejoice, O fervent helper of the Christian race!

Kontakion VIII

A strange and dubious thing it is for unbelievers to hear how torrents of grace gush forth from thine icon, and that it emitteth the sweet fragrance of life; and we, believing the words addressed by thee to thy newly-painted icon: "My grace and power are with thee!", trust that thy grace is ever with this icon. Wherefore, standing before it with reverence, we kiss it and bow down before it, as though before thee thyself; for the honor rendered to an icon ascendeth to its prototype, and through this icon thy grace worketh signs and wonders for all that have recourse to thee with faith and cry out to God: Alleluia!

Ikos VIII

Having been wholly taken up into the heavens, O Mother of God, yet in thy sacred intercession thou hast not forsaken those on earth; for thou hast maternal boldness before Christ our God. Wherefore, establish the life of the Orthodox in profound peace,

43

and ever grant thy servants all things so-ever which are beneficial, that, magnifying thee, we may chant:

Rejoice, container of the uncontainable One!

Rejoice, bearer of the Deity in all His fullness!

Rejoice, thou who didst put forth the heavenly Ear of wheat!

Rejoice, thou who hast delivered the whole world from soul-
destroying famine!

Rejoice, thou who dost ever mediate for our race!

Rejoice, for thy prayer can accomplish much with thy Son
and God!

Rejoice, thou who didst adopt us all at the Cross of thy Son!

Rejoice, thou who ever showest us maternal love!

Rejoice, mediatress of everlasting blessings!

Rejoice, thou who even in this transient life bestowest upon
us that which is profitable!

Rejoice, our manifest refuge amid all sorrowful circumstances!

Rejoice, certain consolation amid grief!

Rejoice, O fervent helper of the Christian race!

Kontakion IX

Thou hast been shown to be more exalted than any angelic
nature, O all-holy Virgin, for thou didst conceive God in the flesh,
didst contain in thy womb Him Whom no one can contain, and
didst hold in thine arms Him Who holdeth the whole world in His
hand. Wherefore, magnifying thee as more honorable than the
cherubim and more glorious beyond compare than the seraphim,
on thine account we cry out to God: Alleluia!

Ikos IX

We see the most eloquent of orators as dumb as fish because of
thee, O Mistress, for every tongue knoweth not how to praise
thee worthily, and even a supernatural intelligence is at a loss
how to hymn thee, O Theotokos. Yet as thou art good, accept the
cry of the angel from us that cry aloud to thee:

Rejoice, thou who art full of grace!

Rejoice, for the Lord is with thee!

Rejoice, thou who art blessed among women!

Rejoice, thou who hast found grace with God!

Rejoice, thou who gavest birth to the Savior of the world!

Rejoice, Mother of the Son of God!

Rejoice, thou who bore the eternal King!

44

Rejoice, thou who budded forth for us the Fruit of life!

Rejoice, thou who wast sanctified by the Holy Spirit!

Rejoice, thou who wast overshadowed by the power of the Most High!

Rejoice, faithful handmaid of the Lord!

Rejoice, for all generations call thee blessed!

Rejoice, O fervent helper of the Christian race!

KONTAKION X

Desiring to save many from the evils, sorrows and afflictions which befall us, O Mother of God, thou hast given us thy wondrous icon, because of which the blind recover their sight, the lame walk, the paralyzed rise up, the possessed are healed, fertility is imparted to the earth, men are delivered from deadly plagues, and cities and homes are saved from fire. Wherefore, glorifying God Who bestoweth upon us such mercies, we cry aloud to Him with fervor: Alleluia!

IKOS X

Thou art a rampart of defense for the Russian Church, O Theotokos, the bulwark and glory of its hierarchy, and the strengthening of the Orthodox faithful against every foe. Wherefore, giving thanks unto thee, we cry aloud:

Rejoice, thou who glorifiest them that glorify thee!

Rejoice, thou who puttest to shame them that refuse to honor thee!

Rejoice, frightening away of the enemy!

Rejoice, deliverance from foreign invasions!

Rejoice, glory of kings!

Rejoice, strength of warriors!

Rejoice, tower and rampart in the day of battle!

Rejoice, life-bearing garden which dost gladden the hearts of the faithful in days of peace!

Rejoice, weapon which the demons fear!

Rejoice, oil of salvation which anointest the wounds of repentant sinners!

Rejoice, our sure hope!

Rejoice, our certain trust!

Rejoice, O fervent helper of the Christian race!

KONTAKION XI

Falling down before thine icon and lovingly kissing it, O

Mistress, choirs of virgins offer thee hymnody of praise and thanksgiving, leading a calm and peaceful monastic life under thy mighty protection; and having placed all their hope in thee, they joyously cry out to God: Alleluia!

Ikos XI

We see thy precious icon as a candle which receiveth a flame, O all-holy Mistress; for, having received the immaterial fire of thy grace, it lighteth new lamps in the copies thereof, which partake of the same power of grace; and it shineth with miracles, guiding to the path of salvation all that cry out to thee thus:

Rejoice, Bride unwedded!
Rejoice, divinely chosen maiden, Virgin Mother!
Rejoice, good instructor of immaculate virginity!
Rejoice, preserver of them that are zealous for purity!
Rejoice, boast of women!
Rejoice, magnification of virgins!
Rejoice, help of widows!
Rejoice, thou who watchest over the orphaned!
Rejoice, feeder of the poor!
Rejoice, vesture of the naked!
Rejoice, consolation of the grieving!
Rejoice, gladness of the sorrowful!
Rejoice, O fervent helper of the Christian race!

Kontakion XII

Wishing to bestow grace upon them that honor thee with love, O Theotokos, thou didst leave the power of grace which resideth in thee in thy holy icons; for the divine grace which abideth with such icons ever worketh signs and wonders, and granteth healing of infirmities of body and soul to all that approach them with love, through thine unceasing divinely maternal prayers to God in behalf of them that cry out to Him: Alleluia!

Ikos XII

Hymning thy wonders which were wrought of old and continue to be worked at the present time, we praise thee as a life-bearing well-spring of grace, as an inexhaustible river of wonders, and as an abyss of mercy and compassions; and placing all our trust in thee, after God, in this life and in that which is to come, we cry out, glorifying thee:

Rejoice, hope of Christians which cannot be put to shame!
Rejoice, haven of salvation for the faithful!

46

Rejoice, hope of the hopeless!

Rejoice, salvation of the despairing!

Rejoice, laver which washest the conscience clean!

Rejoice, dew which revivest the soul!

Rejoice, speedy and free healing of sicknesses!

Rejoice, quick deliverance from all misfortunes!

Rejoice, comforter amid every sorrow!

Rejoice, thou that savest sinners from the abyss of perdition!

Rejoice, relief on the day of death!

Rejoice, our only hope even after death!

Rejoice, O fervent helper of the Christian race!

KONTAKION XIII

O all-hymned Mother, who gavest birth unto the Word Who is more holy than all that are holy: accept now this little entreaty, and for the sake of the magnitude of thy goodness and the depth of thy compassions, be thou not mindful of the multitude of our sins, but fulfil our petitions which are beneficial to our souls, bestowing health of body and salvation of soul, delivering us from all want and grief, and making heirs to the kingdom of heaven of all that faithfully cry out to God! Alleluia! Alleluia! Alleluia!

This Kontakion is read thrice, whereupon Ikos I and Kontakion I are repeated.

PRAYERS TO THE ALL-HOLY THEOTOKOS READ BEFORE HER MIRACULOUS ICON OF KAZAN'

PRAYER I

O all-holy Lady, Mistress Theotokos! Falling down before thy precious and wonder-working icon with fear, faith and love, we beseech thee: turn not thy face away from them that have recourse unto thee. Entreat the Lord Jesus Christ, thy Son and our God, O merciful Mother, that He preserve our land in peace, that He confirm the rule of our lawful civil authorities, that He maintain His holy Church inviolable, and deliver it from unbelief, heresies and schism. For we have no other help, we have no other hope than thee, O all-pure Virgin: thou art the almighty helper and aid of Christians. Deliver thou all that pray to thee from sinful falls, from assault by evil men, from all temptations, sorrows, sicknesses and tribulation, and from sudden death.

47

Grant us the spirit of contrition, humility of heart, purity of thought, correction of our sinful life, and remission of transgressions, that, hymning thy mighty works and thy mercies manifested over us here on earth, we may be accounted worthy also of the kingdom of heaven, and may glorify there, with all the saints, the all-honorable and majestic name of the Father, and of the Son, and of the Holy Spirit, unto the ages of ages. Amen.

PRAYER II

O all-holy Mistress Theotokos, Queen of heaven and earth, who art more exalted than the angels and archangels, and art more honorable than all creation, O pure Virgin Mary, good helper of the world, confirmation of all people, and deliverance amid every need! Look down now, O most merciful Lady, upon thy servants who pray to thee with compunctionate soul and contrite heart, falling down before thee with tears and venerating thy most precious and healing image, asking help and assistance. O most merciful and pure Virgin Theotokos, who art full of lovingkindness! Look upon thy people, O Lady, for we sinners have no other help than thee and Christ our God Who was born of thee. Thou art our aid and intercession, thou art the defense of the oppressed, the joy of the sorrowful, the refuge of orphans, the protectress of widows, the glory of virgins, the gladness of them that weep, the visitation of the sick, the healing of the infirm, the salvation of sinners. Wherefore, O Mother of God, we have recourse unto thee, gazing upon the most precious image of thee holding the pre-eternal Infant, our Lord Jesus Christ, on thine arm; and we offer compunctionate hymnody unto thee and cry out: Have mercy on us, O Mother of God, and fulfil our petition, for all things are possible for thy mediation: for unto thee is due glory, now and ever, and unto the ages of ages. Amen.

This Akathist Hymn was previously published in *Living Orthodoxy*, Vol. VI, No. 4. Both it and the liturgical Service are also available as part of a loose-leaf complete Menaion and collected Akathist series in progress.

Published by
The Saint John of Kronstadt Press
Rt. 1 Box 171; Liberty, TN 37095 USA
ISBN 0-912927-13-5

Wholesale accounts, please inquire
concerning terms and titles in print

Living Orthodoxy,
bimonthly journal of Orthodox spirituality
sample copy $2.50